i be, but i ain't

MW00396108

i be,

but i ain't

Aziza Barnes

YESYES BOOKS

i be, but i ain't © 2016 by Aziza Barnes

Cover Art: ruby onyinyechi amanze,
tenderhearted crosses the sea | 2014
Ink, photo transfer, graphite, pens | 14 x 17 inches
Two Bridges and a Lagos Sea | 2012
Photo transfers, ink, metallic pigment, enamel, florescent marker, colored pencils, graphite, porcelain slip | 42" x 68"
Cover & interior design: Alban Fischer

All rights reserved. No part of this book may be reproduced
without the publisher's written permission, except
for brief quotations for reviews.

First Edition, 2016; Second Printing
ISBN 978-1-936919-39-0
Printed in the United States Of America

Published by YesYes Books
1614 NE Alberta St
Portland, OR 97211
yesyesbooks.com

KMA Sullivan, Publisher
Jill Kolongowski, Managing Editor
Stevie Edwards, Senior Editor, Book Development
Alban Fischer, Graphic Designer
Beyza Ozer, Deputy Director of Social Media
Amber Rambharose, Creative Director of Social Media
Phillip B. Williams, Coeditor In Chief, *Vinyl*
Amie Zimmerman, Events Coordinator
JoAnn Balingit, Assistant Editor
Mary Catherine Curley, Assistant Editor
Mark Derks, Assistant Editor
Cole Hildebrand, Assistant Editor
Carly Schweppe, Assistant Editor, *Vinyl*
Hari Ziyad, Assistant Editor, *Vinyl*

table of contents

i be, but i ain't

"He who does not see the hand of God in this is blind, sir, blind."

—Confederate General Stonewall Jackson

how to kill a house centipede by squishing it behind a photo of miriam makeba while contemplating various iterations of rigor mortis in my gentrified apartment complex on 750 macdonough street brooklyn, ny 11233

it does appear to be a strain   itself viral   of some design even   violent with symmetry each set of legs
                    leading up to more sets of legs & I don't know   how to greet it   how to
kindly suggest   it get the fuck out my house   or lead me to where it multiplies
is there a nest   of these? a hive of these? what do these call   each   other
when in a large amorphous congregation? do these   fall in   love & mate or
mate & hatch? which   is further from what I know? sometimes I can't tell
the human preference & yes,   it is the farthest thing
from a person though it could   burrow in me if I allowed it or even if I didn't allow it
which makes it exactly like certain human qualities   again burrow thru somewhere
that requires   synapse before a holler out can occur   an ear canal for example a
nostril for   example a non-consenting passage   you   know   the   type
conquered when I am too happy   I catch a fever & have to lie down throw   my arms
into an unbearable position   what we talk about   when we talk about
            the shape we leave this world in & yes,   I suppose I am that interested in the   body
defeated or the body striving   to say something new about itself like
the position saints die in neck craned arms   crossed legs   crossed   how   they   don't
decompose & yes,   part of me is ugly enough to want   to be a saint which means I will
never be a saint never die   with all my limbs neatly drawn & I can't say I'd be an amenable
corpse or that you would know   how to greet me,   me & my two tattoos
perhaps a 3rd   before I'm burnt & thrown & yes,   I hope to be burnt &
thrown   not for any spiritual reason unless   claustrophobia is a spiritual
reason I wake up screaming   from   dreams   of   waking   up   underground
between   Mississippi Ohio Montreal A Thumb, White   & no,   I can't
say I thought of anyone   when I did it when I saw   4   antennae   lead   a   long   insect
across   the wall above   my desk not the base of my wrist
        popping against a paper version of Miriam Makeba her grey   hand on her gray pencil
dress a woman   who sang sometimes   with her eyes closed & sometimes not
& yes, it is this that I find least human to sing without your eyes
                open like sleeping next to someone you love it is a symmetry a faith a nest of this
a hive of this   an amorphous congregation of this   so it is likely easy to kill if you can
locate the source & yes, I thought   when one of the antennae dropped the other left
        to twitch without an audible pattern stuck as a corpse   to a woman who was
often not allowed   to leave or forced to stay very far   from   where   she   began   I   guess
you call that exile which is something I do   understand I thought a colonizer's thought
not   "I'm sorry" or   "I shouldn't have killed it" but   "if I don't kill it
now, how   will I find it again?"

13

mutt

mut/
noun, informal
noun: **mutt**; plural noun: **mutts**

1.

humorous, derogatory
a dog, esp. a mongrel. *a long-haired mutt of doubtful pedigree.*
a bitch & her litter. no resemblance. a litter. a careless exchange
of possessions. one body inside another inside another without source.

2.

a person regarded as stupid or incompetent. *Do not give me orders, mutt.*
a mixed person. *You can be mixed, just don't be mixed up!* half &
half. bi-_____ multi-_____ & other words for emptiness. cavity. not of
teeth. of canyon. erosion. unmaking the notion that stones do not breathe. that anything lasts.

14

we have no conception of bastard

i played michael jackson's Beat It at Elmina & all the ghanaians broke into a chain of muscular events. swallow the chalky discharge jackson into the acid lining your intestines. sweat out your slave

driven funk don't walk around with names you don't understand. your father didn't own your mother. moonwalk. beat your chest & hear tell the hollow contortions of name birthplace

father's face. thump thump crack. this ain't Roots. whachu know 'bout a djembe? shim- shimmy-yah. there's a word for this. jackson isn't sitting well. outside the window of a clinic in ghana

a black crow with a white breast caws toward the Atlantic & eats its own wings. inside: 6 nurses with 6 wigs shout prescriptions at a severely dehydrated african american girl who thinks she's

woken up at a supremes revival concert. baby? love is a white hand crawling up your esophagus to remind you of what you cannot digest. *it was probably the water. the water always gets you at*

first. after your first sickness, you don't get sick. your body remembers. the Atlantic ocean is an intestine. welcome home. i want to love you. you pretty. you young. you thing. are you my

mother? a portuguese cat named jackson stumbled onto labadi & shook his gullet loose of bile reminiscent of Motown-era hangovers. his vessel riding the hump of the Atlantic like it

his bitch beat beat beat it up *what's my name?* listen to a mouth at sea floor open. you are . . . then, a history. intravenous tubes dangled out my veins cousin to the chords of headphones lodged

in my ears. i soaked my feet in Elmina & antibiotic seizing in slave chambers at hands not there. phantom: knuckles on jaw grope on breast thrust deep & wet from behind. i appeared to be

dancing. when kofi asked me mid-trigger-prone-shimmy: *what is "black?"* & I regurgitated the sure-fire cure to any slavery: black is *i gonna go. i finna go. i go.*

i be, but i ain't. i bastard.
i done walked with a name i couldn't shake & now i gone.

the mutt as mudbone

This is the last time y'all will see Mudbone.

— Richard Pryor, Live at the Sunset Strip

They done played me out. Done played me
out again. They done played me

For a Fool. My Mama done raised A Played
Out Me. They done me in

& out I go. The door to my Mama house
close. Close, They love with condition. They need me

to play The Fool. My condition:
played. They scream me out, I

done gone. Already gone, I stay. Played.
A scream. The game is a playa, whole &

undone: he never gone & the points hold measure.
My Mama done the seams & sold my

play over the other side of tomorrow I can't see. See me
a measure done & stayed. A handle ready for pour. More

of me: see. See? The Fool & no clothes. Naked & The Fool
me. Me. Done raised a condition. Need. Never whole

& done out. The points ready for scream. A need:
Tomorrow's Other Side. A promise without seams. More

naked & I can't stay gone. Out of need a played game
over & over. Beg my Mama done out of me. Raised

her rent & naked I step out again. The scream. Walk
back no shoes to a night without pour. The Fool &

his Mama: a need played & handled. Measure done
of seam. Ready? They scream for me & I pull my

hem. Scream & I play The Need. Barefoot & fooled.

how to suck your teeth

Tuan do it daily. At everything folk who try to front like they his mama-on-payroll say. Way he do it: like the swoop cut into his hairline. Curled up & back. Rest of his shape up left to a disrespectful politic. Just say something ain't what he planned for. 4 train stop running. Or running local. Or $1 pizza now wanna be 50 cents more than itself. Or Taj tryna get at you with a compass needle point on 125th & Lex after the 4pm bell go off & coat the hallway with scheduled alarm. Or Tatianna love you last Monday & curse your fade & everything underneath it the next. *Whachu mean?* It come before that. It come before the question & I don't know how come. Maybe the sound would crumple up like a fresh killed roach if it came after our beg for reason & I wish I could tell you better or tell you more but *it just be like that sometime* I tell him & Tuan take all his mouth to one side of his face shove in the water lying flat on his tongue & instead of spit it out yards (which I'm told might be someone else's thing e.g. white) he suck it back up.

i could ask, but i think they use tweezers

the shoulder is   a complicated organ   femoral   artery lymph   nodes
tendons all those joints if   a bullet goes thru you there's also   the clothing   oh
yeah   what did you think I mean if it's just this   then that's different but
if it's two layers of that   those are other impurities the body   does its job just
one   function to release what can't stay he walked into the ER   smiled
I need a doctor   *thanks man* blood stops moving to the big   towns   the brain
is a big town   the heart is a big town the kidneys are   hot
spots like Vegas built   to handle armies on vacation the blood learns   to bend another
way   like the legs of a crane they make bullets different   now-a-days
in the   good-ole-days   a bullet went in and out and   the holes matched now
a   .22   a .38   expands in the body absorbs like a tampon   function
pull in all life   he was ordering drive thru food   McDonalds food not
really food maybe like   french fries maybe like   a Sprite maybe like a #2   things that don't feel
like food in the mornings down   the street from my house   from his mama
house a clog   at the 3rd counter this guy has a gun a gun has   an operation has
composition is orchestral   is an organ of some   complication ephemeral
the bullets   are small a shoulder is innocuous   until you become a nurse
the only   reason he died was   speed   and proximity
but if it's a couple   layers of cloth   well   you have to get that out too

19

"Let us cross over the river, and rest under the shade of the trees."

—Confederate General Stonewall Jackson's final words

descendants

1.

Alpha-Positive

I specter. Tire-iron. Bad end
of a wish bone. I watch my throne

& eat pork in your mother's home:
all manner of swine is mine & I swindle.

I stay nimble as parades of men
with forefathers try to examine my mouth

cupped up like a horse & stretched I flex.
I shine
& stay shinin' til my maker

whose name I covet as my first come back
down & break it down: why he make of me

such garbage? Such inoperable shame?

From a wasteland is my kingdom from a wasteland stay
my mother. She taught me first to screw up & steady mean

mug on the pavement at folks not my kin. I never been
more bitter when I arrived at the day:

my face cannot come down from the hate I contain.

I am a hollow king.

2.

Chaser the Eraser

Who dat? Neon handcuffed. Brilliantly
arrested in purgatory and for what?
Don't matter.

I don't snitch. What had happened was
a lot of shit nobody wanna talk bout.

Like how I'm here in the cold wearing long
johns & faceless. Like how my mother
taught me to not get killed. Why not

don't kill me? Who pocketed the crime &
changed all the jargon? Who in my sleep

unmade my name & my bed? Who dat?

Quit sayin I jacked your sneakers! Quit
sayin anything about a "thief"! Whachu
know bout me?
I cover
I cover but my skin

stay screamin! Who dat anyway?
I'm nobody's son! Watch me race gainst
nothing! Watch nothing win.

3.

Crux the monk: A Meditation

In Africa, I am spat upon
then shunned away from the children
as, "The One That Left."

In the Immigration Office in Accra
I am beaten into a bribe as
"The Uppity American Whore."

In some American currencies, like The South,
I am strung up
as, "The Thief In The Night."

In my own home I attempt nightly
to eat my body alive.

4.

Barshaw Gangstarr Instructions for Initiations

Arm yo'self with disposability
& a first rate trench coat. Steal
any man worth his salt. Then
stir him up as an ingredient.
You will find here life is cheap.
You will find the food tastes bad
& the women are stingy with their
hips. You will find I don't unbuckle
my belt to beat or beat off. You will
not find me because what is hunting?
Stay in your lane & kiss my ring &
remember you ain't shit but runt but
still-beating memory of mama's worst
mistake & daddy's one night itch.
To get with me no guns required. &
fuck what anybody tell you 'bout
a color to wear: this ain't Girl Scouts.
To get with me find your nearest junk yard.
Peep there what burns up.
The incinerators are your
new family. They will teach
you the kind of letting go
you will need to achieve
to be in my crew: to wake up
each day
& survive yourself.

5.

Duchess of Candor

The belt stand for
"forgiveness." It's an
Adinkra symbol but
I found it at the thrift
store on 83rd & Lex
& the lady that owned
it before me said she
got it on her trip to
the Motherland even
tho she white so I wonder
what the hell she was even
talking about. People say
a whole lot of nonsense to me.
When I got these earrings, Unks
or Aunks or UUnks, this lady
in The Village & by Village
I mean Greenwich, you know
funky like that, she say it come from
Egypt where there's like thrones &
aren't I supposed to know better
than to walk around wearing shit
that I don't understand? I just thought
it looked pretty. Reminded me of
someone I thought I met once.

over a plate of inferior greens

there I held a devotion to life   as a game of pronunciation sung   from Tolita Bailey

while   sweeping the matriarchal   floor boards *let's call the whole thing off* & when she

died so followed   my ignorance of what actions   could break a neck

though she killed   our meals with her own hands she could've told me   but didn't tell

me   until the ground was thick   with her the body's parts a

gizzard   to suck on marrow of a man   & the method to break him off

               she may have known what joys   would die   in my hands in

church   what ministers smelled dirt   & restlessness under a God that bore

a striking resemblance to James Brown   wielding incomprehensible constitutions

           that I would burn if I wanted   a woman instead of his permed

 & sequined image whose world   was this even under the swagger

           of 10pm I tried to part my grandmother's hair   into two even caliber pews

                    couldn't make it past the hairline   kept undoing & doing my step

coating it   with ultra sheen this would be my embalming   she died the next morning

heralded   by saints of her own invention unlike   when my grandfather

died & my mom said quietly   *mom is free now* there was a road I refused

to name like the night I set to count   all the hairs in her head

how unending   the finite a head of hair unfathomable as death   her home cooking the

casual & implicit murder   toward nourishment at the repass a woman

           in redhatredskirtredshoesred   fur animal draped across her chest   I

decided   she was my grandfather's side-piece or whatever

they called it then *tomaeto*,

tomahto over my plate of greens that Toilta didn't   gather the neck

           bones' inferior   rind of fat falling   into the grease know where your   food has been

who handles   what goes down & inside   she couldn't tell me

until she told me   her body would flatten away from bone still   covered

in synthetic fabric she a meal   herself confined still

           how the coffin my mama bought is an insult

to how we are fed

it's referred to as the law of diminishing returns

it's profitable to have   an interest in collateral   regression analysis   know better &

know   when something is paying for itself   he could work   like   solar   panels

if you keep him   still if you wired the nerves from his

wrists his jugular behind his knee caps to   other wires the way you

jump   start a car you could channel sustainable   energy I am told shows on Animal

Planet are no longer about   animals they are about Bigfoot   & other hard-to-kill imaginings

I'm saying they might have   a point   if the world's ending we should use our

goods to good use   he could be a power source   like fertilizer or something

nuclear I'm told that fear is emotional   but there's a comfort we can work with create   a monster to

hide   a monster vampires   are all the rage in the 21st century

a sexy lie don't look at me I'm   busy here his profit margin   as a citizen is   low

he probably won't reach 30 with all his   freedoms with   all his hands   open

we are in want   of a stable economy let's stimulate that   if you tell us

how to build him we will be ashamed   & build millions of him   we've done worse

& when it was bad we built a museum & when it was really bad we didn't   hear me out

it wouldn't be   an industrial complex just   an environmental complex good

for the soil & all of that   consider him like a stalk   of wheat now like a stock

of company like Apple   like an arm around your shoulder   trade   this for that

preferred chattel   when I say he I of course mean   a blk he when I say

they   I of course mean more profitable characters lemme pitch it to you lemme

pitch a tent

stab

   stab

stab listen it's better to be hinged   than nailed in that's

coffin-speak but I think it applies here   you just have to expand your thinking a bit he could

keep   the house warm   for $16.00 a month guaranteed keep him

wired &   he will not be a threat to   life life   sounds like this terrible idea

we all agreed on doing   but hey   we're invested   the trick is to buy low sell high look!

look!   over there— a zombie!   looky here— where's your son?

the mutt looks at her polycystic ovaries on a sonogram

They show up black on the television. Been there to feed
for years. I consider christening
all weather with a government
ill of nameless thunder. Hair on my chin
they give to me. I comb up
some sunlight to touch what I don't want
of my face. Anymore
is a measurement. I'm still afraid
of dying on the street. To smoke a first
cigarette in a fashion of wanting
to grow. Atrophy is grow. I learn the word
bear in another language is spelt like
ours. I won't bear any mine. The women
in my family grow tumors before
children. They miscarry.
They piss on what they want
to keep safe. To cut down on:
coffee doesn't help. Alcohol doesn't
help. There's hope if you act
accordingly. In a Thanksgiving photo
from 1946 my great aunts
& grandmother hold a 1/5th
of Jim Beam & a turkey leg.
If I die anyway in the street I want
my children to find the names
for my children. I write
them in the backs of books. *ElBird & Octavia
& Calvin Cornelius IV* & they would've been
a real fourth of something. I won't yield
& I won't yield. I bear every officer. I bear
epithet & eulogy. I bear Crenshaw & 48th. I bless
who never happened. I rake up a 10 foot fence
for my kids with a broken alarm system
in Memphis.

"Always mystify, mislead and surprise the enemy, if possible. And if you strike and overcome him, never let up in the pursuit."

—Confederate General Stonewall Jackson

pulp fiction: part one

I watch a spider weave her web & I am not afraid. Or I am afraid, but I'm not implicated. I'm unsure if she qualifies as a parasite if she is what she eats. I watch movies with Black men seated across from White men at tables having curt philosophies on the subject of pride. Ving Rhames & Bruce Willis in Pulp Fiction Reg E. Cathey & Kevin Spacey in House of Cards Season II. The criminal *Black* seems righteous the *White* appears less criminal on paper but in his morality there's a bleakness in need of some instruction. Do they *White* find themselves needing the opinion of them *Black* who have in their genetic code a means to absolve pride entirely for the sake of living under a tree & not from one—an appendage of? The meetings are always on his *Black* turf (his strip club his Blues 78s his bar his restaurant apartment & all). You don't see what he *White* owns & he looks pitiful in need of further submission—is it a kink? I want chicken & I wonder if that's a tell. I want dick & I wonder if that's a tell. I wet my lips & want pussy & I wonder when I got interested in card games. Spades in particular. Where you need a partner presentation fidelity nervousness & want.

hakiu: u

Urge unbuttons us.
Around our sun urgent turns.
Young ruin. Round. Ours.

pulp fiction: part two

Black hands him *White* a manila envelope & jerks it back *you might feel a slight sting Black* hands him *White* iced tea & *I don't want your guilt money* throws it in the drain. *Black* hands him *White* a plate of ribs hands him a prizefighter to buckle under *White* hands on him *Black* when the table is gone. The table then. If there wasn't one. When there wasn't one. Before I see the web I consider finding a way to kill the spider a spray so we don't touch & we outside. *You my nigga?* Rhames has one elbow on the table & Willis reaches *it would appear so. You want me to play the nigger?* Cathey is on the asking side of the table. Between me & the spider is her own manufacture & I could take a broom to it. The worst she could do is nest in my hair. Desperation is interesting if it remains unfulfilled.

down like a shot

falling into unearthed light or something like that is who I was last night. you brought
me a drink you didn't know the name of & told me I *could get it*. you
not the drink which I downed even though it was my 9th
of the night the drink not you. dancehall. always
dancehall. a manner of movement learned
& not easily lost so I wind my hips
anyway & something is happening
to you. *you bout to start*
some shit & I say *good*. not
because it would be.
I haven't been
touched
in a while.
don't start something you can't finish is maybe the worst advice
I've ever heard as you drop a handful of my ass
thudding down a small flight of stairs.
that's what I am. a small flight
of stairs. a small
flight, down.

pulp fiction: part three

There is a fat sack of permutations for how this meeting can end & I want one in particular. I hear Al Green going all *staying here with you is all I need* & the back of Rhames's head gleams in the pale red of the strip club lax in their Monday morning his band aid sealed firm as if with someone's tongue saline waxed in his wound. They won't throw the table over curse the shirts off their backs make love under the Reverend's plea *you'd never do that to me*. Their hands won't touch when he passes Willis his payment won't fondle the money wrapped loosely in an envelope *whatever you want to do is alright with me*. When he buys Willis's body he doesn't indulge in his latest purchase *let's stay together* & it's odd his aversion to touch what belongs to him now his white muscle a cheap cut of desperate meat. *you my nigga?* & why does he even have to ask.

the mutt misses jouvay by no less than 4 hours

the touch of a man is turning shrill   a cicada's
            final screech   their hard plastic other body falling
dirt bound planting   nothing I sleep & dream   of crowds of flies wake   up grabbing at my
phone for a name
for an hour   a number for the chill behind me before me a jaw
            of the older   stock prehistoric &   reassembled clenches my neck 'til it
            a rivet a screw in a bigger design   what tool am I I wear a skirt &   smile the wide way I
should be easy how scratching
            lotto tickets be I should   consider being a lotto ticket an instant disappointment colored
brightly a tongue   always too far out
            the mouth & caught   los angeles lost 63 trillion gallons of water this year   that is the name
of my home   & what information
can that   provide me regarding how I sleep or   how I love or how
            I lose my keys I fall   asleep to Stokely Charmichael   saying *I was born in jail* the land is
moving   taller   creasing against
opposite   slabs like hands forced into prayer   by the fingertips that friday night I wore   the skirt
            I smiled the wide way the way
            of   deserts in droughts & the guy shoves his tongue in &   here I am not hungry
            this guy this business job this   "I live in Long Island City"
                        this inability to salsa at a salsa club   & I respond to her text
2 hours too late & I am afraid   she won't respond again that I canceled
            too many times for coffee   that being alone is all I want   & after that,

her

my dad asks, "how come black folk can't just write about flowers?"

at sun down
I down a couple

whiskey gingers on contemporary balconies with
well
     meaning

white women who say,
the blues
ever heard of it?
my cigarette
put out clean
before its time
Nervous
     White
Lady smile under

that hard side part   it all

clinking

        in my glass

she's a whole person but we're learning about her

You run menace to my name is the beginning of a sentence that ends with a lie I make about love & how I am above it. Grew accustomed to being the king of I-could-give-a-fuck-about-your feeling but the J train service ends earlier each night & I got sick of extracting my name from my phone. The Kid is out of alignment & my body delivers an ache that has nothing to do with apathy or liquor or someone else's sweat, a saunter out my door. Nah, tonight I'm delirious & afraid of phrasing an honest moment to stand by. Tonight, a white dude body checked The Homie & she shouted *funny how y'all forced us to learn English & you so rarely use it*. The Kid: *I Was Forced to Learn English & All I Got Was This T-Shirt*. You can't fake laughter & that's how come so many folk die of it. Richard Pryor talked about fucking around so much I'd envision all the women he had as suits hung in his closet. Often I confuse futility with imagination. In any case I ain't a punk. In any case I was any case. I didn't want anyone to love me but they could at least keep me around.

"My religious belief teaches me to feel as safe in battle as in bed."

—Confederate General Stonewall Jackson

pronunciation: part one

he tells me in mississippi the only laws broken concern meth & obesity. i'm at the dude ranch listening to a black man from Oxford rap *a genocide is a genocide* his 40 acre ballad. land & we want to put our feet in the dirt alive. this blonde soror wobbles into me *hey* & the drawl hits the rim of her Coors Light *so you're not bi?* her lips are 2 sheets of bible paper *you're nervous? it's cause I'm from Mississippi, right?* i ask her if she has a name i can call her. it's Nancy & she tells me i'm going to have a hard time down here. her shirt is a scarf that falls off every time she shouts *woohoo! she could've been anywhere tonight* the other queer black woman says to me *a Keith Urban concert, anywhere.* my lipstick looks like shoeshine polish on her chin & around us are approximately 7 shrines to white Jesus. *they're mostly ironic* says the mississipians.

in my bed & alone a black thing falls out a crack in my white ceiling, a cockroach that can fly! let's all get in bed with the queer black yankee fuck! her androgynous sex her minstrel shuck shuck all down my chin don't cancel my order ship that bitch back to me live! it got to the point where chattel was less fuckable. consent is the mule we never got. a roach wakes me up by crawling on my arm & a black man in queens new york tells me he's envious *at least he gets to touch you.*

let's lay hands on her said the lord.
let's lay hands on her said the soror.
let's lay hands on her said the black man.
let's lay hands on her said the roaches that could fly.

the clouds can't hold shit

I understand forgiveness but I have no current desire. When I'm at home I sleep in the same bed since I was 8. Same fibers in the mattress. I can't smell her she came before my parents bought the bed princess beds as they were advertised.

If you lift the body or liberate the body it don't matter if you think about their product the product of them if you think about them in terms of multiplication & residual what's left over from their last time touched & by whom.

The grass on our front lawn is brown as I am but we still get it cut. I heard there's a drought but I haven't seen any dead so we won't do anything in the remembrance of anything.

Dream the worst ends in that bed. A white guy in a wool coat in the summer shoots me in the kidneys that kind of thing

where everyone in my dream is actually me. On occasion I text older men that wanting me isn't embarrassing it's a choice & we all choose even

what she did to me back in the day & we choose & we are cruel & stupid but when I wake up in the morning there's a sun & a ritual I didn't lose anything. Everyone was alive.

after we drank the table

A table of bourbon & that's the closest I know you. Every part of me is hungry. Knuckled. Liquored. You're demanding I give you a blowjob & I say *no* & you say *okay*. Over me you're very tall. In life you're very tall. Next to the platter of fried chicken a bowl of my ovaries. Pass them to me. You muscle your elbow into the base. My property runs to red yolk. Poured onto the plexiglass table you weed out all my cysts & tell me *baby this ain't lookin' too great*. The bottles are free. The bottles are empty of lust. They could become weapons. I don't love you. I can't set a table of your name in other nameable things & anyway all the bourbon is gone. *Come here.* A husk of my pressed organ dribbles out the crease of your mouth. I take a walnut & crack it along my molars. Your jeans' zipper declines. I figured prior extractions mute the crack & you missed my entire point. I apply the shell between the roof of my mouth & tongue. A press. It won't make a sound or make you leave. You find the proper knife & carve your pants laid to rest on the table. *You're really the worst when you're naked* I don't say. A spread of fresh jam warm from its host on denim. You want to fuck me. The table sucks outlines of sweat from our hands. I look below my chest plate in the shower & plead with it all. Rupture. Surrogate. Adoption. Through the glass I suggest these as names for the children my body doesn't plan on facilitating. You check your bank account & my skin puckers. You raise your leg to climb in. I shove a round of shaved hair into your mouth. Below the seams on your shirt I stare. Penises are so absurd on the body. A shock of land. I never understood or trusted land. I was born during an earthquake & have a single interest in pressure.

fuck boston: part one

In the next life

I pray you   the one plant

Ain't pollinate.
Sentenced to   consecutive   terms
Unfucked. Dying itself   ill-
equipped   to mend
Your sorry
Ass. For you?
Not a damn I
Got. Look Here. How You
LA boy by
birth
Swolle up   from 63rd &
Slauson   think Your mouth new.
Spit holy like   You done Al
ready fucked me
Up.   Nah.   I know
Your
            whole
                        damn
Name. Knew it moment
After your Line Brutha said of
Them Other Dancing Niggas
At Morehouse, or Them Other
Niggas Who Danced At Morehouse or

            Those Niggas Over There Who Also Dance and Were

Near Me At Morehouse that They was

"...
um...   light   ..."

I go like (cuz I

Know   Face of A Man who

            Don't Know Shit   'bout Knowing
Another Man &   he be proud
To let you know   Real Quick where his Sperm
ain't been nor   ever gonna be as if Err'body
wanna taste
                    when in fact ain't No-
Body ever did check for You or Your Damn
Progeny AnyFuckin'Way)

"you mean
Gay?"

& he go like   "Uh-

huh but that ain't what
Scared me."
            & I damn near

Weep cuz you A Black Man
& you cannot know how
Daily I am bound to keep
You & Your Bullshit from
Fear. But Damn if You Afraid
of Folk That Don't Give Two
Fucks About Scaring You or You
At All. They Ain't Pressed. "I'm glad.

I'm
Glad you wasn't
Scared of Them." &
You Bitch Ass
That You Is   who been know Whom
I've touched   & what
I want   when it ain't   You & Yours
Didn't say a damn thing but
"Let's learn a new line step

Brutha." What   Could You
Know of Kin?   Brutha   How? Brutha What?
The Fuck?   You Mean? You?

You A Miscreant.
A Nigga Not Worth A Nickel
& gas fire Full of Fuck Outta Heres if

I found you on the street,
Pray I done got more Religion or
        Less depending on   how much
        You dig   getting your ass beat

With fervor.

alleyway

As fresh garbage is. As dirt sucked out of a fingernail. As a wall clean of prostitutes. When I am this I am at the mercy of my nakedness. A pillar of undress whose power I do not know how to wield. I watch porn. I study the geometry of limbs splayed. Not the moan but the angle of a moan. I swallow. In this way I am a thief. Sometimes I forget my body & go untouched until I am touched & scream. Sometimes I want to eat my breasts down to their bitter rind & spit them out. I want to be the bitter rind without suck and easily thrown. Easily thrown I want to be the pebble thumbed & wished upon before enveloping the lake I sink in. I sink in you the lake & by lake I mean gutter a water that does not hold me well. Here we are not the bodies our mothers made. If you are to hold me hold me as a gun. Grip me & profit the dark. The unattended purse. The pair of heels darting from us in dull claps sharpening against the concrete as teeth against a stone.

you are here

Life be an inarticulate
beast. Given that whole
situation, I allowed for
a democratic entry. I said
wine? & you said *address?*
& I am comfortable asking
for compacted pleasure in
exchange for information
I know by rote. Weeks later &
after a friend a man tries
to fix my toilet & I bound up
to the pipe drained of function.
What I wear is small around my
chest & he tells me to put on a
shirt in my own damn house. Often
I can't say more about what happened
other than it happened. I strangle
a stain of lemon into my tea I tally
the nothing I've said. You couldn't
know I want you if I've already decided
you've forgotten me. Beg my teeth
into the heinous yellow of a hoarder. Wheat yellow.
Harvest a colony of regret in my gullet. If
I were Ole Dirty I'd be a better version
of my demons. I could say *you a ball of fire*
with no feeling & I could say *I'm not smiling*
I'm just showing my teeth the bent hue of plaque
eclipsing even my own disappointment
in how little I ask for.
A dead man asked for more. & is that
the requirement? I hear my cousin
say piece of ass & 20 year something girls
& crazy crazy & the devil never prosper as a prayer
they don't wake up with their uncles' hands
married to the best hips the hood could stack up.

We all got needs. We all want to be carpenters &
watch the rain not fall in. When you were here
before my broken toilet & tea. Before my cousins
& parades of women's arms souring to mucus & clot
the sun beat hard down my curtain: a yellow
bed sheet hung body-tall. We turned shut our alarms.
Laid full as almost-mothers. Of life was patient.
Until the Metrocards & places to be. If
I were Ole Dirty I'd buy a new toilet & sit it
on top of the broken toilet to never forget
where I came from. I'd have asked you
to cancel your day because I don't
like being stuck with all the women
yelling in my head. & you'd say *Dirt.*
Dirty. Be soil. Not soiled. I wouldn't know
what to grow here.

pronunciation: part two

the blade is in his hand & coming up the back of my neck when he says, *Abbesville is how you would pronounce it*. there's a bale of cotton on a shelf next to 4 basketball trophies next to a TV broadcasting *Soul Plane*. across the street is a Rebel flag waving over a detention center behind a Methodist church on MLK Drive. i miss the simplicity of cartoons. a big sign that reads *JAIL* above one, far from anywhere you could get a haircut or baptism. when black men hit a certain age they're 45 in the face forever & one such man in his gator loafers & no front teeth slides up to me something cool & says *I often find myself in the strip club*. i say *I don't go outside if I can help it*. we are both here paying a man with the surname Isaiah to touch us. blade in hand behind our ears until the cut is clean. on *Soul Plane* the older white dude catches a case presumably his first of seeing a Black woman's ass come down slow into a seat behind the 99 cent store adjacent to the Popeyes. his Jones for discount meat. i've never felt a bowl of cotton in my hands. the plastic command of a basketball trophy means *we made it*. we laid hands on it. a woman naked on a pole then is a bale of cotton. a detention center is a basketball trophy yielded from a harvest of church. the 99 cent store is a blade coming up the neck of sacrificed chicken grease. all the poles we pray to burn perm-like on every MLK mandated Avenue. my hair shorn & ankle bound is void of memory. if the eternal 45 year old in his gators saw fit to lift my hair from where it laid after I paid Isaiah what was his, for the knife, for the pronunciation, that would be another thing I'd never feel.

lonely town city province capital of the world or at least continental usa or at least
brooklyn, the bedstuy/bushwick intersection or at least my building where there are
only families & that one married couple who smokes menthols in the apartment

last night I collected my blanket & coiled
way folks do that's spoonin' up made

myself the little side. Smoked a whole cigarette.
Drank a thimble of red wine (a glass—I'm

trying to be beautiful & it's not working), took off
all my pants. Put them back on. Shuffled (if you

can do that lying down. Anything's possible in
this bedroom this economy with this soundtrack)

looked at my two impossible hands when I went for the
broom, ready to dust up the dust to have something

to touch with purpose & it was right there. On the pulse
of the thistle to my palm that I wanted more wanting. I

wanted your whole body on my whole body! To have my incense
piss you off! Make sneezing a daily battle in our apartment (which

we call our apartment, see what I did there? I our-ed us & you
ain't even real yet) & to release the hostility we throw our light

bills at each other (avoiding the eyes & other paper cut
prone sections of skin) predict how to prank the Con-Ed guy

when he comes to shut that shit down. I don't know who you have
to be. Maybe just here? I'll keep cracking at that undercooked

dinner. That undercooked thought. That underwear I bought
for myself (this ain't no pity shit I was happy to buy that for

me. I suppose) thinking of if you would like it. Of how you'd
look when you first saw me naked. What you would say at

this little ole' brown body, turning around
in your stare. Maybe *hello there. Hello, my*

best idea. Hello, my gentle addict. Quit making
so much smoke. You're harder to see that way.

ezra

pay me what you owe me in properties of remembrance, dude. this do to the mother of my current predicament, a lowly instrument to ritual. the payment in question has a computer, a memory & the nerve to bitch. I am thoroughly addicted to Shakespeare, talk that is the talk of nothing, dreams, the debut of I'd rather be with you, may I unlive the gentle strike of your cotton pickin' hands. Yosemite Sam was a racist & guns endeavor my kid laugh, laugh kin to laugh of baby sister fell asleep head first in her cereal. never mind that we all expiring for real for real. convicted of a lonely vibration, my dear I is, as I lay up under whomever & picture the first of things: seeing my government name in the bible. not my full but my first & I am cut in the subliminal fashion.

I wonder if mama could smell it. that I was in love, unlawful. out of favor & with funk. I'm right here, steady. I'm standing straight back, shadow. I found you one mo' gin, pimpin & I'll be a son of a gun if I could just get that first shot clean. your face & no teeth grin. I'd Yosemite Sam that bitch in my pj's & cornrows. I make fists underneath my desk when I write & jump the bed when I corroborate in the subconscious. if I could do it all again I wouldn't do it all again. I engage in regret-logic for a quick one: beads at the ends of my braids, wind-chime systems of alarm, would vane my mama to that closet you said no eyes could open in. she'd find me & us & me in her blue slip you told me to wear & unlive you. your mama remodeled my mama kitchen which is insulting & I think of you when I eat.

fuck boston: part two

Let's get a little mo' pastoral in This Bitch (& by Bitch I mean Location not Woman or Coward):

Sure the drive to Boston was idyllic
& shit. Saw mad geese hobbling in a row
toward water. Felt it as a parallel to my own reasons
for journey. Out of New York via
The Bronx & my long sleeved shirt was backless:
a Bitch Felt Good (& by Bitch I mean myself not
the entirety of women I represent). You were texting
me but you weren't so important at least not
as important as what you promised to do.
Akinyele (a.k.a fella) said it best on their E.P.
"Put It In Your Mouth."

I think the Uber Driver knew instinctively that Your Place was A Place I Should Not Be Going:

but I had talked it thru with My Homie
over a drink that tasted like PineSol the night
prior & he said The Weekend According To Plan
sounded like a great idea. According To Plan will
be the name of my next all female punk rock group
& our first single will be a song called *Fuck That Crusty Ass Nigga*
in devotion to you. But before I get ahead
of myself let this Bitch breathe (Bitch in reference to
The Story being told not
the Air or My Lungs or My Breasts Above My Lungs).

You said *I forgot The Condom* & I remarked that Duane Reade's The World Over are 24/7

& that there are many things you can accomplish
without swaddling your dick up in latex. I know
perhaps I sound cruel, but let's examine cruelty
for a cute minute: You never did explain to Me
why you couldn't give a Bitch some head (A Bitch

absolutely meaning me) as You had heretofore consented to do.
Told you I could've not gotten head in Brooklyn. Could've
not given head in my own damn house. & yes
I can't front that I did please You. Giving a good thing
is one of the reasons we on this planet anyfuckinway. After you
landed a small dose of yourself in my damn mouth
you reported *I'm just not Emotionally Ready to Do That
Right Now*. Do That meaning lock your head between
my legs & praise. Huh. Wish somebody told a Bitch that.
Told my Mama all about it. She prayin for You.

ode to the flying trash

Yes there have been days I've sat down into an impenetrable loneliness. In that regard I am similar to every fiber owning a name. I can picture the man at the liquor store down Saratoga buying a handle heavy enuf to require additional hold losing the need for a home to mend his body with a wet burn leaving the plastic bag black & unrequired to collide with the vagabond air. I hear a disturbance in the tree 2 apartment complexes down & assume like most animals to find another animal making home in a branch of buds playing with the notion of spring. I look up & see a black plastic bag knotted firmly. Not flag enuf to wave. Not proud but caught. In a tight spot. I've often felt that way. Full of some other thing until it realizes I'm a symptom of a deeper problem.

"God has fixed the time for my death. I do not concern myself about that, but to be always ready, no matter when it may overtake me. That is the way all men should live and then all would be equally brave."

—Confederate General Stonewall Jackson

my dad asks, "how come black folk can't just write about flowers?"

bijan been dead 11 months & my blue margin reduced to arterial. there's a party at my house, a house held by legislation vocabulary & trill. but hell, it's ours & it sparkle on the corner of view park, a channel of blk electric. danny wants to walk to the ledge up the block, & we an open river of flex: we know what time it is. on the ledge, folk give up neck & dismantle gray navigation for some slice of body. it's june. it's what we do.

walk down the middle of our road, & given view park, a lining of dubois' 10th, a jack n jill feast, & good blk area, it be our road. we own it. I'm sayin' with money. our milk neighbors, collaborate in the happy task of surveillance. they new. they pivot function. they call the khaki uniforms. i swift. review the architecture of desire spun clean, & I could see how we all look like ghosts.

3 squad cars roll up at my door & it's a fucking joke cuz exactly no squad cars rolled up to the mcdonald's bijan was shot at & exactly no squad cars rolled up to find the murders & exactly no one did what could be categorized as they "job," depending on how you define time spent for money earned for property & it didn't make me feel like I could see less of the gun in her holster because she was blk & short & a woman, too. she go,

this your house?
I say *yeah*. she go,
can you prove it?
I say *it mine*.
she go *ID?* I say *it mine*.
she go *backup* on the sly
& interview me going all *what's your address—don't look!*
& hugh say *I feel wild disrespected*.
& white go *can you explain that?*
& danny say *how far the nearest precinct?*
& christian say *fuck that*.
& white go *can you explain that?*

I cross my arms. I'm bored & headlights quit being interesting after I called 911 when I was 2 years old because it was the only phone number I knew by heart.

brown noise

We are a fifth
of Hennessy & here. *Y'all don't keep*

y'all dogs on leashes? I say &
see anyway. They don't bite. I know you

are going to ask me about my lips
the mouth behind them. How did they meet?

How did they stay? I know you are going
to leave me, 1/2 naked & barking. I know

you are going to drive me to a street without a name
& spit on the tender of my thigh. I know I am only one

name you've forgotten. *I want to tear them*
you say. I am staring at a dog, her teats dragging

on the gravel. I am tired like that. *How?*
You're in my pants, rooting for an angle of them & I

am laughing. *With your teeth?* I'm picturing you
gnawing at their matte lace, rabid the way pleasure

sickens us. Your hands still. My mouth is wet
& closed. Then the rip crisp as new money. They're

dangling long, hanging by whatever
thread is left. *Do you put your dogs in the pound*

if they bite? I know you are staring
at them, the crosshatching of your shred.

Me: a tremor of meat made more naked.
No, you say. *We shoot them.*

self-portrait as a lily white fist:

Humanness does allow for some prudent bleeding. I am ungloved in a sabbath of spit.
Only the turn of cement can arc Black. I am blue damage. Mother gut & tower.
Truth: we are all for rent. Red lined systems. The door out is green and full.

the mutt debates what it might come down to:

another round of pictures from under the microscope. Betrayal on a cellular level. Piled high a lax clot. Insufficient bullets rounded like capsules so I'm not dead but walk around half gone. Like Pam Grier when she played a woman named Coffy hands slain up in twine. Afro deflated & void of glory. I've taken down my razors & stand without weapon in front of you. I look at your pictures. You let someone inside. Told them to chew you up until you couldn't breathe just to be in their warm mouth. Look at you. Barnacled like that as if you went on some great voyage & neglected to invite the rest of me. The white blood cells ain't much better. Overrun with apology & disease. I wish I could leave you like I always do when love arrives & is dressed down for the party. Pam Grier as Coffy wore very few articles of clothing but it was in agreement with the rest of her, a disguise until the suit. You undress me. You embarrass me. Requirements of love: relax. Relax. The house is on fire. Relax. You are not the house even if you built it & I didn't build this that I live in. That I breathe into & beg a painless summer. What I want is hope. Is irrational. Is rationed down to small cleaves found on the ends of tea leaves. Stupid notes that read *love is your greatest strength*. In a day I can take up to 12 pills before I feel like a sick person. We all do things we wish could be done in silhouette. My pills. My blood. Y'all fuckin' up. I'm fuckin' up. I stare down at you from the glass screen & know you're not mine. Pam Grier's Almighty Afro was a wig stuck on her head like an amulet. Sometimes watching that movie I'd want to laugh at her. *That ain't your hair! Those ain't your words! You even know how to shoot a real gun?* Real ain't enough. It strain & ration. It sneak close up & tell it like it is what you is. It ain't Coffy talking a round of smack & high kickin a pimp. It Pam, quiet in her apartment. Icing her face from a beating. It me, sitting still with my blood running but not out. Not fast.

the woman in my head who reflects on our damn near getting shot in fort
greene the first real ass day of summer:

honey, chill.
find yourself
a woman
bent up just like you.
find that ledge &
jump off. on some
see if I care shit. you
care. you researching
miracles but how come your dishes can't make they
way out the sink? sheeyt.
I got a handful
of bullets
just like you.
ain't more midnight trains
to Georgia to find your
piece of mind.
chew cud until you
do the dougie with
Legba at the crossroads.
sell your soul
for a piece
of her mind.
*baby, can I change
your mind?* so many
weddings to attend &
brocades to fixate
your gaze upon.
up on her, you'd
like to be
but he called you his
partner
his *wife*
& you can't sit here
tell me you ain't felt nothin'. there was bullets
under them plastic

cups as y'all walked past the
police blockade. he coulda been the
black man you wept
for this year. 2013: Bijan.
2014: everyone after.
you smart. able
to distinguish gun-
pop from firecracker & you
too chicken shit to pen down
that you might could have
died
on that street corner.
I mean you was
there an' all.
walked real slow past them cars,
& your people. sweetness,
just cuz they black
don't mean they belong
to you.
what white man sold
you that?

watching couples take selfies makes me anxious

Watch them: set the perfect angle. Wrist cocked, short-lived discomfort for the satisfaction result begets. Position the amount of light able to collect on their joint faces. Their smiles hinged & high. Shit looks like taxidermy. They're so perfect I assume they're already over.

you're a woman & I'm a woman
who's into you. I dug a man
recently & he well I don't really
know what happened is happening
& everyone wants to go to fucking lunch.

.

people want to go to lunch at the most unholy hours.

.

he asked if he was
the first person I've had sex with in my bed.
he wanted to know if he mattered & I didn't allow him.
he was. the worst
thing I could've done would've been to say that soft &
honest. in his face. my body open & over his.

.

he hurt my
damn feelings. I said
we looked alike. That it was like fucking myself.

.

woman I could care deeply about
I swear
I won't bring this man with us to lunch.
anyway we aren't going.
you're not hungry.

.

1pm is a great hour to be alive & also
around people. any other
time is subject to what you ain't
saying. everyone is hungry. I save
money so I can go outside.

·

my feet hurt.
I don't have children
so this ache is not noble.
it's a loneliness & when I lie
down nothing.

·

the other day I smoked a cigarette & the smell
lingered on my right hand
when I rested my chin. I recoiled at the intimacy.

·

they write too many songs
about this part. I have
a friend who loves going
on dates. says he feels charming
& shit. on a date
I already want to be in my bed
with or without you.

·

alone & at night
is a juncture I can't
force myself inside sleep.
can't avoid my body, electric
& untouched.

a good deed is done for no good reason

you are a slab   of wood & an unused nail you are   each one & you are them
both you lay   in a Home Depot perhaps or   an architecture firm perhaps
even   in the back of some shed in   Indiana   or   Bogalusa   or
314 7th Street Brooklyn New York without the   industry   of   human   hands
you are just   yourself & no one has made you   into a house or even
said the word   never whispered in your ear   the   possibility
of shelter never   took   a Polaroid of a family & said, "this is something you could keep
warm,"
so you don't know really what could come   of you but you know in the rain   you rust
& mold respectively & one day   a hand is hovering above you   a hand   is   hovering
above you & you   are staring at it   considering the endless permutations
of a hand all its wants   & before long you know the hand is going   to   pick
you up   & you are worried you are a fleet   of pigeons rascaling
your talons in the dirt you are thinking "if I move   I would be beautiful
but I would be moved"
& suddenly the hand   is holding you   the hand is holding you & you are becoming
something   else & you are not fantasizing   a   floor   board's
quality of life   the pros & cons   of assembling into a chair in fact you aren't
thinking much   of anything not asking   the scary questions not   *what if all I*
am   *is all*   *the houses I'll never live in?* or   *if no one walks*
inside, will I be   *a house at all?*   because somehow you know   you are
not a dead   bouquet of miscellaneous daisies from 2 valentines & a heartbreak ago   you
are still possible   the way a set of cheap   crappy
books & a smile a small portion of it   given can be evidence the world won't leave
you   behind so you allow yourself to become
whatever these hands will make you   & when you are   asked how it felt
the day you were suddenly   a house you will not   remember much you will not be able
to define it in words   all you will know is
you did have definition   you were held & you weren't   love exactly
you didn't offer that nature   to last to be a monument marble crafted into the
face   of some president suited & gone   because among other
elements   you were not marble you were never going to be & you weren't a
necessity really   weren't   two cuts   of a branch learning the
arithmetic of fire   unraveling to dust   for a worthy cause like warmth or   survival   you
were   a moment the way laughter   the way breath behind a kiss is you   weren't

dire   but you were the difference an empty lot then a house   then an empty lot as

before   & you know this part that you   won't last that you will be torn   back down

to your simple   self you may in the process   forget what you were

until   you are again   what you were a slab of wood

     a nail & no intention   only you are different now you are

touched you have been moved   made & unmade   swiftly   you have been lived in

notes & acknowledgments

Immense thanks & appreciation to the following journals for publishing these works:

a brief description
haiku:u
the mutt misses jouvay by no less than 4 hours . . . . *PANK October 2014 Queer Issue*

alleyway . . . . *Callaloo Volume 37, Spring 2014*

we have no conception of bastard . . . . *pluck! Fall 2013*

descendants . . . . *Winner of the 2013 NYU Gallery Prize for Radical Pressence*

i could ask but i think they use tweezers
it's referred to as the law of diminishing returns . . . . *Union Station, Issue No. 11, Spring 2015*

a good deed is done for no good reason . . . . *Phantom Limb, Emerging Poets Issue*

the clouds can't hold shit . . . . *Neplantla Review, Summer 2015*

self-portrait as a lily white fist . . . . *The Cortland Review, Spring 2015*

my dad asks "how come black folk can't just write about flowers? . . . . *Winner of the 2015 Winter Tangerine Award for Poetry*

ezra
how to kill a house centipede by squishing it behind a photo of miram makeba while contemplating various versions of rigor mortis in my gentrified apartment complex on 750 macdonough street brooklyn new york 11233 . . . . *The Offing, Spring 2016*

thank yous

thank you my dad Craig Barnes, my mama Marchelle Bailey, my big little sister Sarita Barnes, Sebastian Rivera, Stephanie Barnes, Gary Stephenson, Priti Parkash, Uncle Calvin, Auntie Kiki, Cousin Janelle, Danielle and Anna Lisa, Cousin Taina, Mustafa and Miguel, and every cousin I got from LA to NY and back.

thank you my New York School kin (who I've met there, even if y'all ain't from there): Jerriod Avant, Jeremy Clark, Morgan Parker, Saeed Jones, Ocean Vuong, Eduardo C. Corral, Rachel Eliza Griffiths, Dennis Allen II, Kevin R. Free, Lauren Whitehead, Adam Faulkner, Angel Nafis, Shira Erlichman, Rico Fdk, Mahogany Browne, Jive Poetic, Audrey Hailes, nichi Douglas, Chinaza Uche, Dan & Kaz Safer, Ani Taj, Emily Bass, Thomas Gibbons, Alex Albrecht, Danika Brown, Sunny Hitt, Justin Perez, Geoff Kagan Trenchard, Samantha Thornhill, John Manuel Arias, Anthony McPherson, Nora L. Carroll, Natyna Bean Osborne, Christopher Gabriel Nuñez, Jayson Smith, Nabila Lovelace, Camonghne Felix, Safia Elhillo, Ladin Awad, Yarminiah Rosa, Arielle John, Desiree Bailey, Jon Sands, José Olivarez, Bob Holoman, Danez Smith, Machel Ross, Hannah Kallenbach, Hugo Picciani, Paul Tran, Tonya Ingram, Michelle Jackson, Thiahera Nurse, Natalie Elbert, Josh Smith, Nicole Terez Dutton, Joshua Bennett, Carvens Lissant, Jorge Luis Brito, Nate Marshall, Diamond Sharp, Phillip B. Williams, Syretta McFadeen, Lynne Procope, Cornelius Eady, Dawn Lundy Martin, Jess X. Chen, Jason Lalor: thank you. for every eye, hand & hour on my work, in my life. thank you Poets House Fellowship & my kin: Rachel Eliza Griffiths, Paul Tran, Ricardo Hernandez, Andrinikki Mattis, Esther Lin, Rio Cortez, Yanyi Lao, Timothy Ree, Vikas Menon, Aldrin Valdez, Stephen Motika, and Joe Fritsch. thank you. thank you. thank you. thank you Cave Canem Workshop in Brooklyn, where all the madness began: Erica Hunt, Camonghne Felix, Jayson Smith, Nabila Lovelace, Mahogany Browne, Najee Omar, Nadia Alexis, Joyce Lee Ann, Charleen McClure. thank you. thank you. thank you. thank you Callaloo: Vievee Francis. thank you. thank you my divine fabrics, the other halves of my heartbeat: Safia Elhillo, my brother. Camonghe Felix, my wife-from-another-life. Sean Mega DeVinges, the trillest DJ in the land. thank you. since day one, thank you. thank you my Poetry Gods, Poet Linc partners, & brother kin always: Jon Sands, José Olivarez. thank you always. thank you my Southern-partner-in-crime & forever up to something: Nabila Lovelace. thank you. thank you. thank you.

thank you my Mississippi kin: Derrick Harriell aka Uncle Trill (for editing my work even before I moved down), April Harriell aka Auntie Trill, Kiese Laymon, Eve Dunbar. thank you. thank you. thank you. y'all kin & made me feel like the South is a place I could live & thrive. thank you to my workshop kin Jan Veberkemos, Marty Cain, Andrew Friemann, Amy Irwin, Sarah Srgo, Matt Kessler, Maggie Woodward, & Ann Fisher Wirth, Beth Ann Fennelly, & every comment & every hand laid upon this work: thank you.

thank you LA homies: Christian Washington, Stan Washington, Karen Washington, Chasen Washington, Alexa Velasquez, Taylor Simone, Jamal Harris, Maya Humes, Jasmin Harvey, Venessa Marco, Shihan Van Clief, Beau Sia (for reading my poems when I was 17 & really needed someone to read my poems. thank you immeasureably), Jeremy Radin, Daniel Lisi. thank you.

thank you Danez Smith. for nominating this work. for creating space. for being the trillest & always showing love. thank you. thank you YesYes Books team: KMA Sullivan for her brilliant eye, hustle & the hour long phone calls from day one. thank you Jill Kolongowski. thank you Heather Brown. for the immeasurable work you do, for your kindness and brilliance and badassery. thank you Alban Fischer for your incredible work on this cover, this font, all these choices that made this book gorgeous. thank you Stevie Edwards, Amber Rambharose, Phillip B. Williams. thank you ruby onyinyechi amanze for saying yes to our using your artwork. thank you for *tenderhearted crosses the sea*, for *Two Bridges and a Lagos Sea*, and for your graciousness, beauty and overall blk girl magic. thank you again Morgan Parker for bringing us together. thank you. thank you.

also from yesyes books

Full-Length Collections

The Feeder by Jennifer Jackson Berry

Love the Stranger by Jay Deshpande

Blues Triumphant by Jonterri Gadson

North of Order by Nicholas Gulig

Meet Me Here At Dawn by Sophie Klahr

I Don't Mind If You're Feeling Alone by Thomas Patrick Levy

If I Should Say I Have Hope by Lynn Melnick

Some Planet by jamie mortara

Boyishly by Tanya Olson

Pelican by Emily O'Neill

The Youngest Butcher in Illinois by Robert Ostrom

A New Language for Falling Out of Love by Meghan Privitello

I'm So Fine: A List of Famous Men & What I Had On by Khadijah Queen

Gilt by Raena Shirali

American Barricade by Danniel Schoonebeek

The Anatomist by Taryn Schwilling

Panic Attack, USA by Nate Slawson

[insert] boy by Danez Smith

Man vs Sky by Corey Zeller

The Bones of Us by J. Bradley

    [Art by Adam Scott Mazer]

Frequencies: A Chapbook and Music Anthology, Volume 1

    [*Speaking American* by Bob Hicok,

    Lost July by Molly Gaudry

    & *Burn* by Phillip B. Williams

    Plus downloadable music files from

    Sharon Van Etten, Here We Go Magic, and Outlands]

Chapbook Collections

Vinyl 45s
A Limited Print Chapbook Series

After by Fatimah Asghar
Inside My Electric City by Caylin Capra-Thomas
Dream with a Glass Chamber by Aricka Foreman
Pepper Girl by Jonterri Gadson
Bad Star by Rebecca Hazelton
Makeshift Cathedral by Peter LaBerge
Still, the Shore by Keith Leonard
Please Don't Leave Me Scarlett Johansson by Thomas Patrick Levy
Juned by Jenn Marie Nunes
A History of Flamboyance by Justin Phillip Reed
No by Ocean Vuong

Blue Note Editions

Beastgirl & Other Origin Myths by Elizabeth Acevedo

Companion Series

Inadequate Grave by Brandon Courtney
The Rest of the Body by Jay Deshpande